THE VIKINGS

NEED YOU!
- KINGS • RAIDERS •
- SHIPBUILDERS • FARMERS •
- RUNE-MASTERS • SKALDS •
- BLACKSMITHS • TRADERS •
- LAWSPEAKERS • WEAVERS •
- EXPLORERS • THRALLS •

AND MANY MORE JOBS AVAILABLE
APPLY AT THE THING

ALL IN A DAY'S WORK – RAIDERS AND TRADERS
was produced by **David West** **Children's Books,**
5-11 Mortimer Street, LONDON W1N 7RH.

Consultant: Dr Richard Hall
Illustrators: Studio Boni-Lalli-Critone-Pieri and
Francesca D'Ottavi (Virgil Pomfret Agency),
Francis Phillips, Ken Stott (B.L. Kearley Ltd)

First published in Great Britain in 1997 by
Heinemann Children's Reference, an imprint of
Heinemann Educational Publishers, Halley Court,
Jordan Hill, Oxford OX2 8EJ, a division of Reed
Educational and Professional Publishing Limited.

MADRID ATHENS
FLORENCE PRAGUE WARSAW
PORTSMOUTH NH CHICAGO SAO PAULO MEXICO
SINGAPORE TOKYO MELBOURNE AUCKLAND
IBADAN GABORONE JOHANNESBURG KAMPALA
NAIROBI

ISBN 0-431-05384-7 (HB)   ISBN: 0-431-05385-5 (PB)

British Library Cataloguing-In-Publication Data.
A catalogue record for this book is available from the
British Library.

Printed and bound in Italy.

ALL · IN · A · DAY'S · WORK

RAIDERS
AND
TRADERS

ANITA GANERI

Heinemann

CONTENTS

INTRODUCTION

Welcome to the Viking world! You've gone back in time more than 1,000 years and arrived in Scandinavia – Denmark, Sweden and Norway – at the height of the Viking Age. Join a Viking raiding party, plundering monasteries for loot. Watch a shipbuilder at work or stop to listen to a poet telling tales of gods and kings. See a duel being fought in the Thing. Or buy a beautiful silver brooch from a master craftsman in the market. Read on to discover other jobs people did. Will you find the job for you?

YOUR PLACE IN VIKING SOCIETY DEPENDED ON HOW RICH OR POWERFUL YOU WERE.

1. KING OR CHIEFTAIN – SUPER-RICH AND POWERFUL

2. JARLS – VERY RICH NOBLEMEN AND LANDOWNERS

3. KARLS – NOT-SO-RICH FREEMEN SUCH AS FARMERS, CRAFTSMEN AND FISHERMEN

4. THRALLS – POOR SLAVES

A T THE START OF THE VIKING AGE, each village had its own local chieftain. Later, each country had its own king. Being king brought plenty of perks. You had your own army to order about, and your own poet to sing your praises. You lived in a splendid hall, wore the best clothes, drank the best beer and ate the finest food. And when you died, you got to be buried in your best boat.

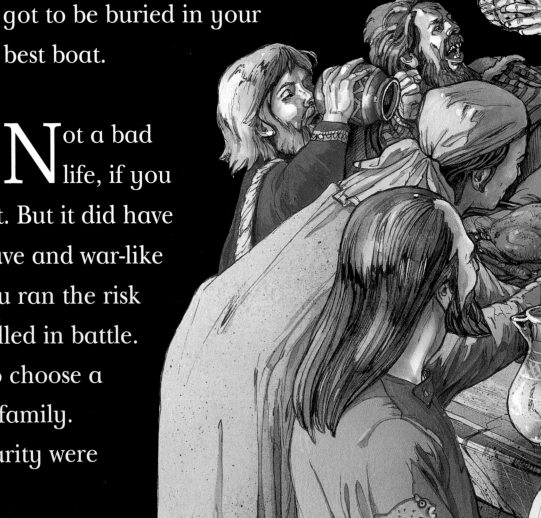

Not a bad life, if you played your cards right. But it did have its down side. Being brave and war-like was all very well but you ran the risk of being wounded or killed in battle. Then the people had to choose a new king from a noble family. Age, health and popularity were all taken into account.

JOB DESCRIPTION: HIGHEST RANK IN THE LAND. LUXURY ACCOMMODATION. REGULAR FEASTS.

PAY: LIMITLESS LOOT AND PLUNDER.

DID YOU KNOW?

The Vikings were very fond of nicknames. One of their chieftains was called Ragnar Hairy Breeches after his furry trousers. His wife made them specially for him to keep him safe from dragons!

FOUR VICIOUS VI-KINGS

ROLF THE GANGER
(860-928)

VIKING CHIEFTAIN. CALLED THE GANGER, OR 'WALKER', BECAUSE HE HAD TO WALK EVERYWHERE. HE WAS JUST TOO LARGE FOR A HORSE TO CARRY. BANISHED FROM NORWAY FOR STEALING CATTLE.

ERIC BLOODAXE
(C 905-954)

KILLED HIS HALF-BROTHERS TO BECOME KING OF NORWAY. NOT VERY POPULAR. OVERTHROWN BY HARALD FINEHAIR. FLED TO YORK. STILL NOT POPULAR. KILLED IN AN AMBUSH.

HARALD BLUETOOTH
(C 910-985)

SON OF GORM THE OLD. FIRST KING OF ALL DENMARK. BECAME A CHRISTIAN AFTER SEEING A MISSIONARY PICK UP A RED-HOT IRON BAR WITH HIS BARE HANDS. OVERTHROWN BY HIS SON, SVEIN FORKBEARD.

CANUTE THE GREAT
(C 990-1035)

SON OF SVEIN FORKBEARD. RULED DENMARK, THEN ENGLAND. BROUGHT PEACE AND PROSPERITY. WISE AND JUST. FAMOUS FOR PROVING THAT HE COULDN'T HOLD BACK THE SEA.

One of your kingly duties was to hold lavish feasts which could sometimes last for two weeks at a time!

WANTED!

Brave, loyal
volunteers wanted
to join a
raiding party
Destination:
Ireland
Looting and pillaging
guaranteed.
Past experience preferred.
Apply to: Olaf the Lucky
By the Great Fjord
'May the godheads grant
you luck.'

THE VIKINGS WERE BRAVE WARRIORS and fierce fighters, famous for their lightning raids along the coasts of Europe. Wherever they went, they spread panic and fear. At first, their prime targets were churches and monasteries, with rich pickings of gold and treasure, and monks to be sold as slaves. Later, they raided towns. In fact, raiding is how the Vikings got their name. The word 'a-viking' means to go raiding or looting.

JOB DESCRIPTION: SEASONAL WORK OVERSEAS. A CHANCE TO MAKE A NAME FOR YOURSELF.

PAY: GET RICH QUICK! EQUAL SHARES OF LOOT FOR ALL.

To a Viking warrior, courage, honour and glory in battle were all. Dying in battle was the very highest honour. Only then could you enter Valhalla, the Hall of the Slain, in Asgard, the home of Odin, Thor and the other gods. Here you lived a great life – fighting all day and feasting all night.

DID YOU KNOW?

The fiercest Viking warriors were called 'berserks'. In battle, they fought in a frenzy, showing no signs of fear. The word 'berserk' still describes someone who behaves wildly or recklessly.

Warriors were full-time soldiers, or farmers who spent a few months of the year raiding, then returned to their farms.

To BE A VICTORIOUS VIKING RAIDER you needed one thing above all else – a longship. The Vikings were brilliant at building ships and specialist shipbuilders were in great demand.

Longships were made of wood cut from the forests. They were about 18 m long. They had large woollen sails, striped red or blue and white, and oars for rowing when the wind dropped. The prow (front) was carved in the shape of a dragon or snake, designed to scare your enemies.

JOB DESCRIPTION: HIGHLY SKILLED WORK IN TOP PROFESSION. PROMOTION IF YOU PERFORM WELL.

PAY: SKY'S THE LIMIT FOR MASTER BUILDERS.

DID YOU KNOW?

Rich Vikings were sometimes buried in their longships, together with furniture, weapons and even slaves. If you couldn't afford such luxury you might have to make do with a humble rowing boat.

BUILD A VIKING LONGSHIP

1. MANY MONTHS BEFORE, THE TIMBER IS CUT DOWN AND STORED. THE BEST SHIPS ARE MADE OF OAK AND PINE. IT TAKES TWELVE TREES TO BUILD A LONGSHIP.

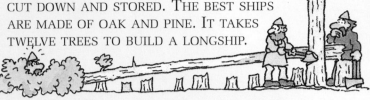

2. THE SHIPBUILDER CHOOSES A TALL, STRONG TREE TRUNK FOR THE KEEL (BACKBONE). TWO CURVED PIECES OF WOOD ARE JOINED TO THE ENDS. THE FRONT ONE IS CARVED INTO A FIERCE DRAGON HEAD.

3. THEN LONG PLANKS OF PINE ARE ADDED TO THE KEEL TO BUILD UP THE BOTTOM AND SIDES OF THE SHIP. EACH PLANK OVERLAPS WITH THE NEXT.

4. NEXT, RIBS AND CROSSBEAMS ARE FITTED INSIDE THE SHIP. THE PLANKS ARE NAILED OR TIED ON TO THEM.

5. ANY GAPS ARE PLUGGED WITH WOOL OR ANIMAL HAIR, DIPPED IN STICKY TAR, TO MAKE THEM WATERTIGHT.

6. HOLES ARE CUT IN THE SIDE FOR THE OARS. THEN THE RUDDER AND MAST ARE ADDED.

7. LAST BUT NOT LEAST, THE SHIP IS NAMED. WHAT ABOUT GREAT DRAGON, OR LONG SERPENT, OR RAVEN OF THE WIND? TAKE YOUR PICK!

THE FISHMONGERS' NEWS

FISHMONGER SEEKS ASSISTANT. OWN MARKET STALL. MUST BE CLEAN, PUNCTUAL AND HARD-WORKING. TRAINING GIVEN. GOOD PAY AND PERKS, INCLUDING UNLIMITED **FREE FISH.**

Depending on where they lived, Vikings hunted reindeer, polar bears and whales and fished cod, herring, salmon and trout.

DID YOU KNOW?

Onions were used in porridge. If a warrior was wounded, he would eat onion porridge. If you could smell onions through the wound, the wound had pierced his stomach and he would die.

W HEN THEY WEREN'T OFF RAIDING or exploring, most Vikings worked as farmers. They grew grain and vegetables and gathered fruit. They raised cows, goats, sheep and pigs. You would feed your family, then sell any extra at market. The whole family helped on the farm. Unless you were very rich and could leave the hard work to your slaves, of course.

JOB DESCRIPTION: HARD BUT VARIED OUTDOOR WORK. OPPORTUNITIES FOR WORKING ABROAD.

PAY: BOOST YOUR INCOME BY SELLING EXCESS AT MARKET.

You ate two meals a day – breakfast and dinner. Ordinary Vikings ate fish, meat, bread and goat's cheese, washed down with beer. Poor people made their bread from a mixture of dried peas and pine bark – it was very tough and chewy!

THE FARMING YEAR IN ICELAND

AS FARMING LAND BECAME SCARCER AT HOME, MANY VIKINGS WERE DRIVEN OVERSEAS. IF YOU SAILED TO ICELAND ...

1. CUCKOO MONTH (APRIL-MAY)

 THE SNOW MELTS. YOU PLOUGH YOUR FIELDS AND SOW BARLEY AND OATS. YOU ALSO DIG PEAT AND CUT WOOD FOR FUEL.

2. EGG TIME (MAY-JUNE)

YOU COLLECT SEABIRD EGGS FROM THE COAST AND SHEAR YOUR SHEEP.

3. SUN MONTH (JUNE-JULY)

 YOU MILK YOUR ANIMALS AND MAKE BUTTER AND CHEESE. THIS IS ALSO THE BEST TIME FOR MAKING LONG JOURNEYS.

4. HAYMAKING MONTH (JULY-AUGUST)

YOU MOW THE FIELDS TO MAKE HAY. EVERYBODY HELPS.

5. CORN-CUTTING MONTH (AUGUST-SEPTEMBER)

THE CORN IS HARVESTED.

6. AUTUMN MONTH (SEPTEMBER-OCTOBER)

YOU ROUND UP YOUR COWS, SHEEP AND GOATS FOR WINTER. SOME ARE KILLED FOR MEAT. THERE ARE FEASTS AND CELEBRATIONS.

7. WINTER (OCTOBER-APRIL)

WINTERS IN ICELAND ARE LONG, COLD AND DARK. YOU WORK INDOORS, MENDING YOUR TOOLS, MAKING WARM WINTER CLOTHES AND REPAIRING SAILS. YOU CATCH UP WITH YOUR CARVING AND WAIT FOR SPRING.

DID YOU KNOW?
According to legend, Odin, the king of the gods and the god of wisdom, risked his life to bring the runes back from the Land of the Dead and present them to the Vikings.

THE VIKINGS WROTE IN LETTERS CALLED RUNES. These were made of straight lines so they were easy to carve on wood, bone or stone with a knife or chisel. You didn't have pens or paper. The Viking alphabet was called the futhark, after the sounds of the first six runes. There were only 16 basic runes so some stood for more than one sound. Confusing!

The Vikings used runes in all sorts of ways. You couldn't write them yourself. You had to hire a rune-master to carve them for you.

Being a rune-master was a good, steady job. There was always a need for your skills. And you could travel around the country with your work.

JOB DESCRIPTION: HIGHLY SKILLED CAREER FOR NEAT, ARTISTIC TYPES. REQUIRES A STEADY HAND.

PAY: GOOD RATES PAID BY SATISFIED CUSTOMERS.

WRITING WITH RUNES

THERE WERE MANY WAYS IN WHICH RUNES WERE USED:

1. ON RUNE-STONES SET UP AS MEMORIALS TO BATTLES AND DEAD RELATIVES OR TO SHOW OFF A PERSON'S GOOD DEEDS.

2. FOR WRITING THE OWNER'S NAME ON PRECIOUS BROOCHES AND RINGS, SILVER CUPS OR JEWELLERY BOXES.

3. FOR MAGIC SPELLS, CURSES AND CHARMS. IF YOU WERE ILL, YOU HAD A SPELL CARVED ON A PIECE OF BONE. YOU KEPT THIS UNDER YOUR PILLOW IN THE HOPE THAT IT WOULD HELP YOU TO GET BETTER.

4. ON MILESTONES FOR ROADS, AND ON MARKER TABLETS FOR BRIDGES AND BOUNDARIES.

5. YOU MIGHT HAVE YOUR NAME CARVED ON YOUR SWORD TO BRING YOU LUCK (OR STOP YOU LOSING IT!)

6. EVEN IN VIKING TIMES — AS GRAFFITI ON WALLS AND STATUES!

TODAY ONLY — A RARE PUBLIC PERFORMANCE BY EGIL SKALLAGRIMSSON, THE GREATEST POET OF HIS AGE. RECITING HIS LATEST WORK IN PRAISE OF KING HARALD AND HIS GREAT DEEDS.

ADMISSION FREE
'NOT TO BE MISSED!'
(ORM GORMSSON, POETRY CRITIC FOR THE DAILY VIKING)

THE VIKINGS MIGHT HAVE BEEN BIG, MEAN AND TOUGH but they loved a good poem – the longer, the better. Professional poets, called skalds, were hired to entertain the king and his guests at court. They told poems in praise of the king's heroic deeds. Many kings took their own personal skalds into battle. King Harald Hardraada (Hard-ruler) of Norway took ten!

So if you had a good memory (as nothing was written down) and a way with words, being a skald might be for you. Flowery language was a must. For example, a battle became a 'reddening of the spears', blood was 'wound dew' and slaying your enemies was 'feeding the ravens'. Luckily your audience knew what you meant!

JOB DESCRIPTION: CANDIDATES FROM GOOD FAMILIES ONLY FOR PRIVILEGED PROFESSION.

PAY: GOLD AND A GOOD REPUTATION AWAIT THE BEST.

The down side of the job was that you were expected to break bad news or give difficult advice to the king. No one else dared. It was thought to sound better in verse!

DID YOU KNOW?

The great poet, Egil Skallagrimsson, once saved his life with some quick thinking and a long poem. He was captured by his deadly enemy, Eric Bloodaxe, and sentenced to death. But the vain king was so flattered by Egil's dazzling verse that he spared him.

The Terrible Tale of Sigurd, the Dragon Slayer

The Vikings loved stories of dragons, gods and heroes. This was one of their favourites ...

'Once upon a time, there was a dashing hero called Sigurd the Volsung. Sigurd killed the evil dragon, Fafnir, with a sword forged by the dragon's own brother, a dwarf called Regin. But Regin turned against him. He plotted to kill Sigurd and seize all the dragon's gold himself. The birds tried to warn Sigurd but he couldn't understand them. Then, while Sigurd was roasting the dragon's heart, he accidentally drank a drop of its blood. Now he could hear the birds' warning words. Quick as a flash, he grabbed his sword and chopped the dwarf's head clean off.'

FOR TOP-QUALITY SWORDS

VISIT
SVEN THE BLACKSMITH
THE OLD FORGE
MARKET STREET
HEDEBY
(THE LAST WORKSHOP IN TOWN)
GUARANTEED RUST-PROOF AND
TO LAST A LIFETIME.
'FOR SHARPNESS YOU CAN
REALLY FEEL'

I F YOU WANTED A QUIET LIFE, with a steady income, you might have learned a craft. Most Vikings were good with their hands. But specialist craftsmen, especially blacksmiths, were greatly admired. After all, they were responsible for making swords – a warrior's most prized possession. Some blacksmiths worked in towns. Others travelled the country, selling their goods and doing running repairs. You learned your trade from your parents or from another family nearby.

MAKE A VIKING SWORD

1. THE BLACKSMITH HEATS SEVERAL THIN IRON BARS IN THE FIRE UNTIL THEY ARE RED HOT.

2. THEN HE TWISTS THEM TOGETHER AND HAMMERS THEM FLAT TO MAKE A STRONG BLADE.

3. HE WELDS ON TWO STRIPS OF FINEST STEEL TO GIVE THE BLADE SHARP EDGES.

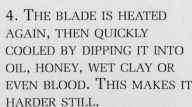

4. THE BLADE IS HEATED AGAIN, THEN QUICKLY COOLED BY DIPPING IT INTO OIL, HONEY, WET CLAY OR EVEN BLOOD. THIS MAKES IT HARDER STILL.

5. THEN IT IS FILED AND POLISHED SMOOTH. A FINE SWORD MUST HAVE A FINE HANDLE (HILT). THIS IS MADE OF WOOD OR BONE.

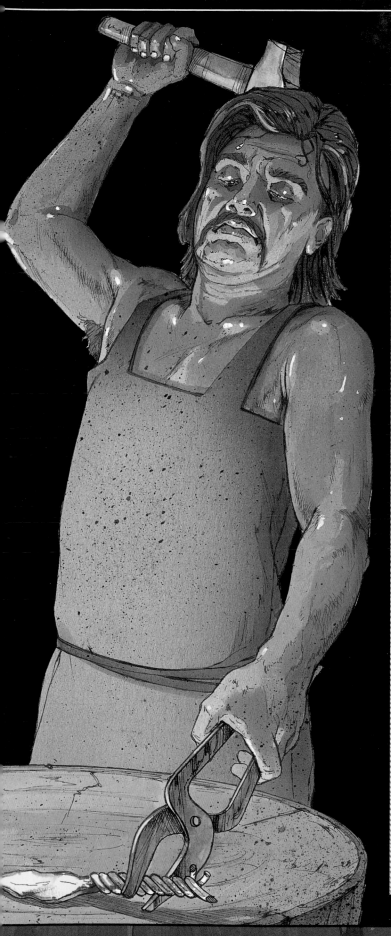

EIGHT CRAFTY VIKINGS

1. JEWELLER
THE VIKINGS LOVE JEWELLERY AND USE BROOCHES OF GOLD, SILVER OR BRONZE TO PIN THEIR CLOTHES. THE RICHER YOU ARE, THE FANCIER YOUR JEWELS.

2. COMB MAKER
ALL THE VIKINGS HAVE LONG HAIR WHICH NEEDS REGULAR COMBING. THE COMBS ARE CARVED FROM RED DEER ANTLERS.

3. SHOEMAKER
SHOES ARE MADE OF CATTLE HIDE WITH LACES OR ANTLER TOGGLES. FOR WINTER WEAR, SOME HAIR IS LEFT ON FOR EXTRA WARMTH.

4. BEAD MAKER
THE VIKINGS LIKE TO WEAR BEADS. THEY MAKE THEM FROM COLOURED GLASS, AMBER AND JET. SCRAP AND BROKEN GLASS ARE OFTEN RECYCLED AS BEADS.

5. WOOD CARVER
VIKING ARTISTS CARVE FABULOUS BEASTS TO DECORATE HOUSES, SHIPS, WAGONS, FURNITURE AND SLEDGES.

6. BONE CARVER
THE BONE CARVER MAKES KNIFE HANDLES, PINS, NEEDLES AND PLAYING PIECES FROM BONES AND ANTLERS. HE ALSO MAKES DRINKING HORNS FROM HOLLOW COW HORNS.

7. MONEYER
MONEYERS WORK IN THE TOWN, STAMPING COINS FROM STRIPS OF SILVER.

8. SOAPSTONE WORKER
SOFT SOAPSTONE IS CARVED INTO BOWLS, COOKING POTS AND MOULDS FOR MAKING METAL OBJECTS. IT IS OFTEN USED INSTEAD OF POTTERY.

SILVER AND SLAVE TRADER
SEEKS TRUSTWORTHY
PARTNERS TO SHARE COSTS
FOR A FORTHCOMING
TRIP TO RUSSIA.
HAS OWN SHIP AND CREW.
GUARANTEED PROFITS.
CONTACT BJORN THE SWEDE
TENT NO 3
BY THE HARBOUR

IF YOU LIKED TRAVELLING and had a head for figures, you might become a merchant. You could grow rich trading slaves and fur for silver in Russia. Or bringing walrus ivory, bearskins and seal-hide ropes from the frozen north. The south was best for luxuries such as glass, wine and silk. Merchants also took food supplies to the Viking settlers in Greenland and Iceland.

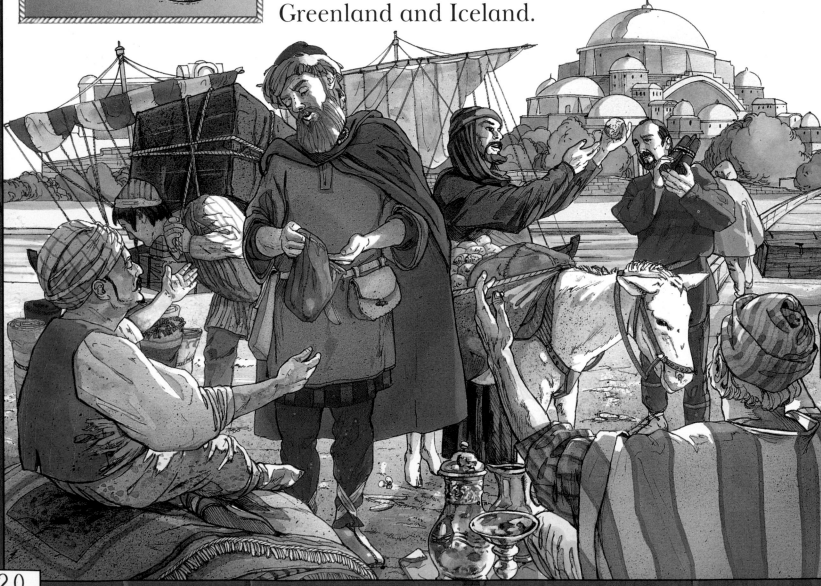

JOB DESCRIPTION: GREAT OPPORTUNITIES FOR ENTERPRISING TYPES IN EXPANDING BUSINESS.

PAY: EXCELLENT PROFITS AND PROSPECTS.

Markets were held in the large Viking towns and this is where you sold your wares. Goods came from far and wide, even from Arabia. Buyers paid a very good price (in silver) for amber and for slaves. While in town, you stayed in a tent by the harbour. Then it was back to your ship for another voyage.

People paid for goods with goods of their own, or with chopped up bits of silver jewellery or coins. This was called hacksilver.

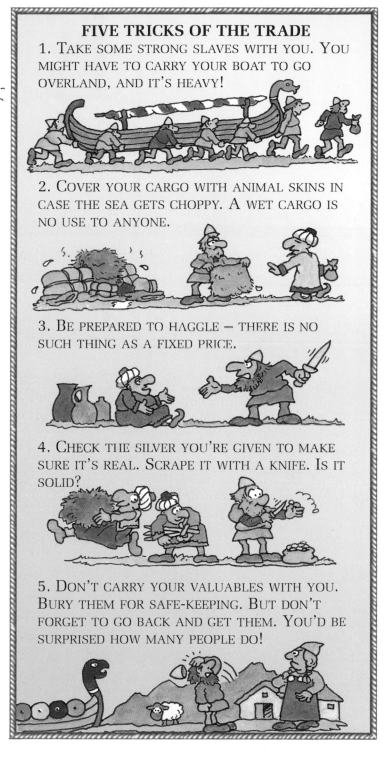

FIVE TRICKS OF THE TRADE

1. TAKE SOME STRONG SLAVES WITH YOU. YOU MIGHT HAVE TO CARRY YOUR BOAT TO GO OVERLAND, AND IT'S HEAVY!

2. COVER YOUR CARGO WITH ANIMAL SKINS IN CASE THE SEA GETS CHOPPY. A WET CARGO IS NO USE TO ANYONE.

3. BE PREPARED TO HAGGLE – THERE IS NO SUCH THING AS A FIXED PRICE.

4. CHECK THE SILVER YOU'RE GIVEN TO MAKE SURE IT'S REAL. SCRAPE IT WITH A KNIFE. IS IT SOLID?

5. DON'T CARRY YOUR VALUABLES WITH YOU. BURY THEM FOR SAFE-KEEPING. BUT DON'T FORGET TO GO BACK AND GET THEM. YOU'D BE SURPRISED HOW MANY PEOPLE DO!

Every merchant had a handy set of folding scales to make sure he was getting his money's worth.

PUBLIC ANNOUNCEMENT

Calling all freemen
of Iceland!
The next annual meeting
of the Althing will begin
next Thursday on
Midsummer's Day
at
Thingvellir
(Parliament Plain)
Camping available

Each Viking community had an assembly, called a Thing. All freemen had a say in the Thing. You passed laws, decided whether to go to war and tried criminals. If you'd fallen out with your neighbour, the Thing was the place to settle your differences.

Iceland had its own assembly, called the Althing. It met every summer, for two weeks. Everyone had to attend. A group of chieftains, led by the lawspeaker, was elected to judge criminals. They heard the evidence and then announced what the punishment was to be. Criminals were fined, banished, sent into slavery or made to do difficult tasks. Each year, the lawspeaker recited part of the law to the crowd. Nothing was ever written down.

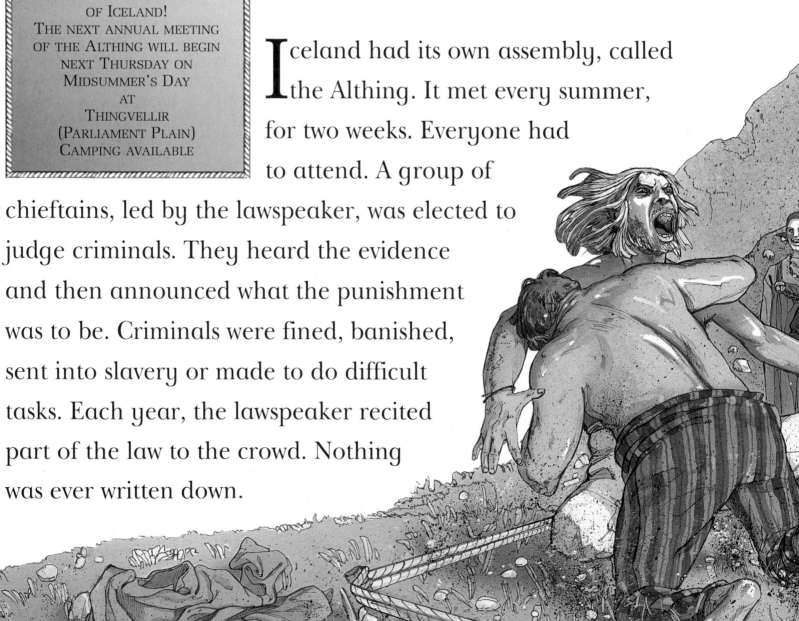

JOB DESCRIPTION: RESPONSIBLE PUBLIC POST IN CHARGE OF LAW AND ORDER.

PAY: NONE. IT'S A VOLUNTARY POSITION.

Your honour and good name were all important. If someone insulted your family, you might challenge them to a duel. If you killed your opponent, you won. If you both survived, the man with the most sword wounds was the loser. He had to pay you in silver.

DID YOU KNOW?

The Vikings believed that everyone and everything had a price. A murderer had to pay his victim's family a fine, based on the dead man's worth. In Iceland, a freeman was worth 120 ounces of silver. You were charged less if you only cut off someone's nose.

The lawspeaker stood on a special rock so everyone could hear him.

Your whole family attended the Thing. There was plenty to do, including horsefighting, wrestling and bareback riding.

23

MEET GUDRUN. She's the wife of Leif Olafsson. At the moment, Leif is off a-viking so Gudrun has to run their home and farm. She makes sure that all goes smoothly until Leif returns. Viking women were quite independent, for their time. They could own land and property in their own right, and get divorced from their husbands. Importantly, they had the keys to the locked chest where the family kept its valuables.

A large part of Gudrun's day is spent weaving. She has just finished a new sail for her husband's longship. She also makes woollen clothes, blankets and wall-hangings. First she spins the wool or flax (to make linen). Then she weaves the cloth on a loom.

She also teaches her daughter to cook, bake bread, brew beer, milk the cows and to use weapons in case the farm is attacked.

JOB DESCRIPTION: CREATIVE, PRACTICAL WORK. SUITABLE FOR FULL-TIME HOUSEWIVES.

PAY: NONE. BUT YOUR FAMILY APPRECIATES YOUR EFFORTS.

MOST VIKING WOMEN WERE KEPT BUSY AT HOME. BUT SOME HAD UNUSUAL PROFESSIONS.

1. RUNE-CARVER
RUNE-CARVERS WERE USUALLY MEN. BUT ONE WOMAN RUNE-CARVER IS KNOWN FROM THE SAGAS.

2. ANGEL OF DEATH
RATHER A GLOOMY JOB. AN OLD WOMAN WHO HAD TO STRANGLE ANY SLAVE GIRLS WHO WERE TO BE BURIED WITH THEIR OWNERS.

3. VALKYRIE
FEMALE WARRIORS SENT BY ODIN, THE KING OF THE GODS, TO CARRY THE SOULS OF DEAD WARRIORS TO VALHALLA.

4. QUEEN
ONE FAMOUS QUEEN WAS QUEEN ASA, THE MOTHER OF HARALD FINEHAIR. SAID TO HAVE MURDERED HER HUSBAND AND GOT AWAY WITH IT.

5. AND FINALLY ...
AUD THE DEEP MINDED DIVORCED HER HUSBAND, KING OLAF THE WHITE OF ICELAND, AND RETURNED TO THE HEBRIDES. WHEN HER SON DIED, SHE WENT BACK TO ICELAND AND STARTED HANDING OUT LAND LIKE A CHIEFTAIN.

PLOT 1

DID YOU KNOW?
You could divorce your husband if he took to wearing girly shirts or even showing too much bare chest! Your husband could divorce you if you wore trousers!

BORED WITH LIFE? LOOKING FOR ADVENTURE? Why not sail away to a new life? The Vikings were very daring explorers – especially the Norwegians. They sailed right across the North Atlantic Ocean to Iceland and Greenland. They even got as far as America, hundreds of years before any other explorers. Many took their wives and families (and their animals) with them, and settled in these new lands. It was getting too crowded at home.

You needed to be a good sailor. The journeys were dangerous and long. Many ships were lost in storms. And you didn't have a map or compass to guide you. You relied on the stars and Sun instead. You also followed birds, shoals of fish, and landmarks, such as islands and mountains.

JOB DESCRIPTION: A CHANCE TO SEE THE WORLD. MUST ENJOY ADVENTURE AND HAVE A SENSE OF DIRECTION.

PAY: DEPENDS ON WHAT YOU FIND.

THREE ACE EXPLORERS

1. ERIK THE RED

NATIONALITY: NORWEGIAN
OCCUPATION: CHIEFTAIN
FAMILY: WIFE, THJODHILD; SONS, THORVALD, THORSTEIN, LEIF; DAUGHTER, FREYDIS
DISTINGUISHING FEATURE: RED HAIR AND A FIERY TEMPER.
CLAIMS TO FAME: BANISHED FROM NORWAY FOR MURDER. SETTLED IN ICELAND. BANISHED AGAIN IN 982 FOR ANOTHER MURDER. EXPLORED AND SETTLED IN GREENLAND. HAD A SAGA WRITTEN ABOUT HIM.

2. BJARNI HERJOLFSSON

NATIONALITY: NORWEGIAN
OCCUPATION: SEA CAPTAIN
CLAIMS TO FAME: FIRST EUROPEAN TO SEE AMERICA IN 986 WHEN HE LOST HIS WAY IN THE FOG WHILE TRYING TO SAIL FROM ICELAND TO GREENLAND TO JOIN HIS PARENTS. SOME FOG! BUT HE DIDN'T GO ASHORE.

3. LEIF ERIKSSON

NATIONALITY: NORWEGIAN
OCCUPATION: EXPLORER SON OF ERIK THE RED
NICKNAME: LEIF THE LUCKY
CLAIMS TO FAME: BOUGHT BJARNI'S BOAT AND FOLLOWED HIS ROUTE. LANDED IN AMERICA IN ABOUT 1001. CALLED IT VINLAND, AFTER ITS GRAPE VINES. VIKING SETTLERS DIDN'T STAY LONG. THEY FOUGHT WITH THE LOCALS AND WERE DRIVEN AWAY.

Explorers used sturdy ships, called knorrs.

DID YOU KNOW?

Erik the Red named Greenland Greenland. He wanted to make it sound attractive to settlers. He didn't think they would want to go there if they knew it was rocky, windy and icy! And it worked – hundreds of Vikings followed him there.

SLAVE AUCTION
FOR THE BEST SLAVES IN TOWN
TRAINED IN COOKING,
CLEANING AND ALL HOUSEHOLD
CHORES
PAYMENT IN SILVER ONLY
ON VIEW AT THE SLAVE MARKET
BIDDING STARTS 9AM
THURSDAY

IT WAS BAD LUCK IF YOU WERE BORN A THRALL, or slave – the lowest of the low. You might have to work on a wealthy man's farm, doing all the worst chores. You had very few rights. You couldn't own land or carry weapons. And you didn't even get to vote in the Thing.

Not all slaves were born slaves. Many were prisoners captured in raids. Monks were highly prized. They were taken to market and sold to the highest bidder. You could also trade slaves for silk, furs and luxuries.

DID YOU KNOW?
This is how one Viking poem unkindly described a thrall:
'Wrinkled hands and knobbly knuckles,
Fingers thick and face foul-looking,
Back bowed down, and big flat feet'!

JOB DESCRIPTION: ALL THE HARDEST, DIRTIEST JOBS. VERY FEW PERKS.

PAY: NONE. YOU MAY BE ABLE TO BUY YOUR FREEDOM WITH EXTRA WORK.

If your owner was kind, he might grant your freedom. Or allow you to buy it by working extra hard. Then he might give you a small plot of land on his farm. Other freed slaves became servants or craftsmen.

A SLAVE'S DAY

1. YOU GET UP AT THE CRACK OF DAWN. YOU STOKE THE FIRES — IT'S VERY COLD.

2. YOU MAKE THE BREAKFAST (AND EAT SOME SCRAPS). THEN YOU FEED AND CLEAN OUT THE ANIMALS.

3. YOU SPEND THE MORNING BOILING UP SEA WATER TO GET SALT FOR SALTING MEAT AND FISH FOR WINTER.

4. IN THE AFTERNOON, YOU DIG PEAT FOR FUEL. AND YOU SPREAD DUNG ON THE FIELDS. VERY SMELLY!

5. WHEN YOU'VE MILKED THE COWS AND GOATS, IT'S TIME TO MAKE THE DINNER.

6. WHAT A TIRING DAY! YOU'RE GLAD WHEN IT'S TIME FOR BED — EVEN THOUGH IT'S ONLY STRAW ON THE FLOOR.

GLOSSARY

Berserks

The most feared Viking warriors. Fought wildly and bravely in battle.

Duel

A fight, usually to the death, to settle an argument or punish someone for a crime.

Futhark

The Viking alphabet. It was named after the sounds of the first six runes (letters).

Jarl

A rich Viking nobleman or landowner.

Karl

A Viking freeman (not a slave). Karls worked as farmers, merchants and craftsmen.

Knorr

A merchant's ship. Broader and sturdier than a longship, with more room for storing cargo.

Longships

Long, narrow Viking warships. Also called dragonships.

Odin

The king of the Viking gods. He was also god of battle, poetry and wisdom. He rode a great, eight-legged horse called Sleipnir.

Rune

A letter in the Viking alphabet. Runes were carved on wood, stone and pieces of bone.

Saga

A long story told about Viking gods, heroes and kings. The sagas were not written down until the 13th century.

Scandinavia

The region which covers the countries of Denmark, Norway, Sweden and Finland.

Skald

A Viking court poet who recited verses about the courage and great deeds of the king.

Thing

The assembly of freemen which governed a Viking community. The national assembly of Iceland was called the Althing.

Thor

The Viking god of Thunder. He was a larger-than-life figure, fond of feasting and with a fiery temper. He was enormously strong.

Thrall

A Viking slave. Many slaves were prisoners of war.

Valhalla

A hall in Asgard, the home of the Viking gods. The souls of dead Viking warriors were believed to go to Valhalla.

INDEX